For Bob Martin, with respect
for your fine poetry, best wishes!
Dave Marwitz
12/31/04

The Ice-Carver

The Ice-Carver
© Copyright 2004 David Manning
ISBN: 0-9759256-0-1

Longleaf Press
Methodist College
5400 Ramsey Street
Fayetteville, NC 28311

Managing Editor: Michael Colonnese
Editor: Robin Greene
Assistant Editor: Lynda Ward
Layout: Bill Billings
Printing: Monarch Press
Cover Art & Design: © Copyright 2004 by Patricia Roberts

Other Chapbooks by Longleaf Press:
That Echo, Deborah Doolittle, 2003
Los Hijos, Barbara Presnell, 2002
Red Land, Black Land, Tina Barr, 2002
Logic of the Lost, Kenneth Chamlee, 2001
Birth Mother, Joanna Catherine Scott, 2000
Junkanoo: A Christmas Pageant, Keith Cartwright, 2000
Mortal, Judas Riley Martinez, 1999
Lost Languages, Jonathan Minton, 1999
The Tar Baby on the Soapbox, Carole Weatherford, 1999
Unravelings, Barbara Presnell, 1998

*For Doris,
whose constancy
the carver never found—-*

ACKNOWLEDGMENTS

These poems first appeared, sometimes in slightly different versions or with different titles, in the following publications:

Asheville Poetry Review: "The Ancient Chorister"
Coastal Plains Poetry: "Skid Row"
The Comstock Review: "Postcard from Verona"
Crucible: "Mysteries" and "The Ice-Carver"
Free Lunch: "Pegasus"
New Orleans Review: "Perhaps"
Pinesong—The N.C. Poetry Society: "New Issues" and "Red Poppy"
Rattle: "Buddhist Pigeon"
Wellspring: "Old Address Book" and "Trinity Sunday"

"Next" first appeared in *Poets Anonymous*, by David T. Manning, Old Mountain Press, 2001.

I thank Ann Deagon and Rebecca McClanahan who read many of these poems and provided valuable comments.

THE ICE-CARVER

On the promenade deck
of the M/S Tropica, the ice-carver
works against the clock. Intent
as Donatello, he chips into
the block, releases a falcon
flying from the soft blue stone.
He moves swiftly over the ice,
the gathered crowd already
losing focus, melting away
to the next entertainment.

His work complete, the carver
steps back, brushing ice chips
from his beard. In the cloud-light
he could be a young Buonarroti,
chiseled fragments in his dark hair,
recalling David's liberation
from his white stone.

Already the falcon's wings are wet,
and already the bell
for lunch calls the stragglers away.
A movement in the melting mirror
catches the carver's eye—
a white sea-bird vanishing.
The carver's message passes
like a poem never written down.

POSTCARD FROM VERONA

Under the Via Capello archway
to the balcony of Juliet, in every color
of Verona, is a Sistine Chapel
of graffiti: *Baffy + Kurt Insieme*,
Benedetta, alone in blue,
Simona e Giani Forever, mixing
the languages in rose of Titian,
Fiorenza, in gold, *Fernando*,
with stars.
      Someone named *Carmina*
has written:
            Ave mundi luminar
            Ave mundi rosa

      I shine my flashlight
on it, a ceiling of the Vatican
torch-lighted. Here are no guards,
no hours of visit.

            Someone approaches.
            Her red dress rustles
            as she walks.

The wall is soft
to my felt-tip. It is like
marking on an arm.

NEW ISSUES

Waiting in the post-office queue
for the *Virgin and Child* Christmas stamp,
I see the Enrico Fermi issue on display.
The Roman physicist, like a Moses of our age,
chalks revelations on his slate, *carbon*—
star-forged alpha of our flesh, and with us
escaping into space and time. He smiles,
pleased to share good news. I feel
December's chill bite from the swinging door.

Lorenzo Costa's portrait on the other stamp
has caught the blue-clad mother and her babe
in a moment of unlikely serenity. How far
we have traveled since Lorenzo's day!
In this darkening chill, I would return
to his three-tiered world, to cloak myself
against the winds of space in folds of the Pieta,
find refuge in gentle Mary's flowing folds,
bound for whatever awaits beyond the stars.

TRINITY SUNDAY

Gathered into the gloom of bells
we enter, too full of life,
unready for ceremony.
The great organ shouts us down,
roaring the presence of God.

Between forefinger and thumb,
a black-folded man raises
        the tiny cup.
He asks of us strange things,
we give an unworldly answer.
(To some, he must remain a man,
to some, a man has ceased to be.)

Down in the congregation,
unconscious of each other, women
remove their gloves in unison,
preparing to receive the bread of heaven

(then words and bells give each
their choice of what the loaf and cup become)

and it is done.
The great organ blares us back.
To the organist and all
who pray without ceasing,
church and the world are the same.

Out in the street, the day
diffuses before our cinema eyes.
Groping for our old stations,
we reassure ourselves with pleasantries.
The world, too, has a fair argument
whether we believe it or not.

MYSTERIES

You are the music
While the music lasts.
—T.S.Eliot

I light candles to the way
your eyes would find me
from the far choir loft
and you would smile,

      to the day
we brought the smell
of *Liquidamber* leaves indoors
with us, the first two stair steps
wet with the May rain; on a wall
a painting I had never seen—
geese rising from a marsh at dawn—
street sounds with tones,
the green-blue of late afternoon.

How can light so absolute be gone—
no lesson to learn, no explanation?
Only a wall where a door
once opened. A mystery

like death
or where fire goes
when it goes out.

THE CHURCH OF SANTA YSABEL
WAITS AN APPROACHING STORM

*The disappearance of the old bells that hung outside
the chapel of the Church of Santa Ysabel is the
subject of grievous conjecture among Indians and
pioneers.*
—San Diego County history

    Red morning light.
    High south wind blows
    the saltbush flat and sky-light bleeds

    one wrong color into another.
    Now, the sand's rose-quartz
    and blue Russian thistles roll in the gale.

    Over the wind, a cow-bell clatters
    arrival at the road gate of a visitor
    not there. I can't remember

    the story of the church bells—
    were they lost or stolen?
    In the Indian graveyard, plastic saints

    flutter against old stones
    and the little church huddles
    in the warning light like one homeless,

    bracing for the storm.
    Like the one who had nothing
    and even that was taken.

LANCELOT'S DREAM AT CASTLE CARBONEK

Sweet and gamy hay smell
Craft of the darting rain
Found a forgotten stable
Never found again.

There a strange grail found shelter
From hail and the driving water,
Light of life on the rafters

That wind in the sockets made flicker.
Ark of the covenant of life
Traveling with the weather.

Where is that grail-bright stable
Bread and cup on the table?
Gone with the wearying weather,
Gone and the service is over.

RED POPPY

Sovereign and free
as geese rising to the stars, finale

of all arguments for God.
I have seen Him light
a darkened room

with the bright incarnation
of your smile.

           Now
in the shadowed concert hall
you are white
as a desert lily in the night.

You are the forest fire
inside me, you are the blood
red poppy.

THE ANCIENT CHORISTER

The old guy with his nose
full of Vick's has a voice
like a moose in full cry

and breath like an opened grave
but they let him sing
the Messiah year after year.

For His acceptable praise,
God calls up all His instruments—
even the old man,

like a taped-up gym piano
with broken, blackened keys
still an authentic musical species,

he dons his robe again and sings
(and Handel smiles, directing
      from the wings).

SKID ROW

In front of a cheap hotel
the old man takes out his baggage
in the yellow light—an ex-boxer
or waiter or retired pioneer
with that unmistakable
blunt athletic confidence,
dressed for some personal rodeo,
showing the street he is still alive.

Here, old men die in winter
but blue busses pull across the scene.
If there were lights & blankets,
they are gone—
the love & food & church parade moves on.
        Today,

more men are missing
at roll-call on the street
and have gone somewhere to wear
their red ties & Sunday best.

THEY ARE DEBATING MY CASE

in Heaven and I wait
in a dark anteroom,
the deserts of unbelief.

From Lincoln Center, Row 34
I left a shattered audience
in the second act of *Faust*.

This is not what I expected.
I did not float
above my slumped twin,
nor drift through a tunnel
toward some welcoming light.
I came in an eyeblink, awake, alive!

I have peeped into the Kingdom,
through the keyhole of a great door.
I have seen shattered legs made whole,

mastectomies transformed, breasts
ripe as Eve's in her garden,
as Susanna's in her bath. (Once,
I would have looked with lust
upon these, resurrection's fruits). Now

that I have seen proof, is it too late
to believe? Surely I am no worse
than Thomas, who was given a second
chance to convince himself.

Above the arguments, I hear a chorus rising
and long to join. I had no infirmities,
but age and mortality.
And foolish wishes.
I wished to sing *Faust—Salut Demeure*
I wished—to sing high C in Heaven.

GALLERY QUINTET

Adam finds Jill alone in the music room. Her face startles him—he cannot picture her when they are apart. She smiles, and he is lost in white-water from a place he cannot remember. In a far room, a choir is singing *Ave Verum Corpus*.

Randy leans sideways in his desk chair for a better view as Janice shifts her tanned legs. He imagines how they join in their hidden smoothness and digs in his pocket to caress a ribbed and lubricated sheath. He wonders what will happen when they are alone together.

Blinky Rosette has had little to eat since Tuesday. He breaks the plastic seal on the bottle of *White Lady* Angelica with a dirty fingernail, unscrews the cap and drinks, feeling the warmth flow into the caverns below.

The medical examiner snaps on her latex gloves and approaches the cold body on the white enameled table-top. She places her scalpel against the discolored abdomen and draws a delicate red line.

The archbishop uncovers the Host and raises a consecrated wafer. As the bells sound, he feels the Mystery reborn between his fingers and thumb. He thinks of his mother who died last February—the wrinkled backs of her hands.

BUDDHIST PIGEON

On the Bangkok sidewalk, it pecks
a pink gum-smear.
If it has a soul, it's a crapshoot
        whether
its karmic trip is going
up or down. If souls go down,
they may get very small or
have no size at all,
unthinkable as the primordial
zero universe which we
believe, but can't conceive.
In theophysics séance parlors,
one may posit various houses
for the soul, Buddhist, Christian,
otherwise, then ask how
Soul traffics with the Mind
(which I've always pictured as
a skull-sized synthesizer hitched
to Yeats' *dying animal*).
        Perhaps
our pigeon's soul is a
Heifitz of whatever
instrument its journey
takes it through. It may be limited
and singular, lingering beneath
the mauve and lice-infested wings
to animate the worm-brained
bird, or vast and multiple, navigating
flocks in flight. Suppose
this soul is indivisible,
smaller than the smallest thing
and made of nothing else. Finally

it *slips like a dewdrop into the shining sea.*
Each of us—worm, bird or me
just a blink of the brightest light.

AFTER THE FLOWER SERMON, KASYAPA ADDRESSES THE FOREST

The green twig of Buddha
and the dead brown branch of Buddha—
surely, he is everywhere.
Blessed is the sunlight
and blessed the dark where the trail ends.

The lizard shimmering on the cedar log
is Buddha, and the dead squirrel by the path.
Even the fallen flower and the path's stones.

The gray lark that preaches: *Even in death
we are in life.*

Blessed the slender bamboo
and the stout,
the long body of Buddha
and the short.
Blessed his abundance everywhere!

The swallows diving in the air,
and the ants that climb in martial line
cannot escape enlightenment,
for one day's sunlight is their prayer.

This stumbling beetle that pushes
the diamond-body of his dung
and the great owl that shouts in daylight
are the Enlightened One. And the firefly
and the owl's downy-winged mate,
certain as the stream-brightened stones,
as the shaded moss where the path begins.

NOBODY HOME

> *Nothing is more real than nothing.*
> —Samuel Beckett

I think of an airport lobby
suddenly without Muzak,
of a silent supermarket
shoppers stranded with their thoughts

of the hush
ten minutes into
a thirtieth high school reunion
while the band plays on.

The longed-for vacation
was yesterday.
What did we long for
on the long trip home?

In the midst of life we are
in Myrtle Beach.

What animates suburban robots
can be fun
such bubbly immortality—
what can die
that never was alive?

So, *clean well-lighted place*
how do you give such peace?
I think of a world
treading water until
some authentic miracle.

—Italicized quotations are from
the *1662 Book of Common Prayer*
and *The Short Stories of Ernest Hemingway.*

IN OCTOBER

afternoons, sun warms
a hot spice smell in the wind
that quits quick and clean
as a promise broken.

      Only this instant is real
in the warm and light
and the next also
when it comes.

      Wind comes and goes
and shows you
(more than you want)
how every waking moment
      is goodbye.

CHANSON NOIR

There must be a reason for sleek women
to fade, women in black who turn my head
at the click of their heels in corridors.
One would greet me at gatherings for the dead.

At funerals of my friends, she was always there
alone, waiting for me—in her white gloves—
ready with any solace she could give
as I entered those sad, magenta-curtained rooms.

Sometimes, I tried to catch a glimpse of her
adjusting her skirt as she sat in an office chair,
her face, that turned so many faces in dark halls,
gave a soft light, faint smile, streak of a tear.

She was a pin-up made flesh. I knew
only her name and that her children were gone.
She filled my senses despite her innocence
and I was hesitant to introduce her to my own.

In her simple black shift she drove me beyond
lust to terror—yet she reached out to me
at those audiences of the dead with strange mercy,
as if I suffered more loss than I could see.

She retired, then quit her body's discipline,
revealing the tutor she had always been.
Unmasked from her distracting succulence, she taught
how the collapse of flesh turns lust to shame.

PEGASUS

The horse rears skyward as she hugs
his back, nears the live oak's lower
branches. The girl is lost in transport
as she takes the great surge

between her legs. The menace
of trees and ground are only colors
now—dun of road dust, forest green—
fear cancelled by the moment's shine.

So begins their first long gallop.
Ektachrome 200 shows only a girl
flying on a white-tailed colt. What was it
her mother warned her of?

Horse and girl have found a trail
her mother has forgotten
and follow a river whose rising
she will not see again.

PERHAPS

Someone in the photo who looks like me
climbs a spring-wet trail to Alta Peak,
wild columbine—five colors
against the sky. I was never there.

I never swam with Carl at Heather Lake.
Nor was I in Florence—the Ponte Vecchio
in that picture through a rainy mist.

Perhaps I hold memories until
what happened never happened at all—
maybe time abolishes time.

I think of East L.A., thirty years ago—
the TV is on and Dad falls asleep in front
of company. That's where I never was,
so often now.

But those photographs! Two boys
bobbing in some mountain lake—sun
in their eyes, the moment drifting
like cloud shadows over the water.

ONE

Ahead—this field of bronzed Arabians
against the dying sun is like a painting.
        But what of a solitary horse?
Nature does not care
about one of anything, or the horse
who lived here before.

A hawk soars in the high blue.
What of the numbered hair
or the counted sparrow? A flock
of geese has a leader but no soul.
(Still, they turn back when one member
fails in flight.) Species arrive, evolve
in time, and yet they are abstractions,
like histories and future generations—
a *Mardi Gras* of ghosts.

The hawk is a vanishing speck against the sun.
The third person plural is a handful of sand
into the night wind.
Only the death of one is real.

SOL

Driving west
into the open furnace
door of the sun

I think how this
warming, hungry fire
brought us into being,

how, in the far future
it will redden and swell
as if with anger,

consuming us with
our moon dreams. But
sun knows no anger,

He is alpha, omega,
becoming, un-becoming,
giver and taker

of light and life.
Our words will go
with us into his blazing door.

He is the editor,
whose final judgment
is fire.

OLD ADDRESS BOOK

kept too long, so many names crossed out,
phone numbers like weathered dates on stones,
addresses X'd and gone. Such simple cancellation

of lives. I'm afraid to call the old numbers left,
no way to prepare for what I might find after
these years—the sorrow, resentment caught

off-guard, my voice too high and eager,
a curious intruder come back to unearth you
from someplace you'd rather be. Or worse—

to dial up an irritated stranger, your familiar sound
gone like a stone into the sea,
showing how we are all so interchangeable. Listen—

if my voice breaks, it's not from curiosity
but fear—that you are gone. I only want
to find you as you were. And so I will write

again, hoping this year you will answer.
That, like me, you will find the safe ground
of written words between us. If only I could

tell you how some word or glance of yours
once grew in me, became part of what I am.
You will never know the way you are alive in me.

NEXT

Even after good times funnel
down to intervals between waiting rooms
(for another report to set you *free*)

—you'll still come back for more.

After the fiftieth reunion
(where the class president went
unrecognized), you'll wait by your mailbox
for the Kodacolor souvenir.

Someday, reprieves expire
and tomorrow becomes now.
Think of what your molecules have
always wanted and let them go.

Think of how easily TV strangers die
in distant lands. Where do all the people
come from who never heard of you?
How inexhaustible they are!

That's the secret. Think
of yourself as news
from a far country.

BIOGRAPHICAL NOTE

David Treadway Manning, a California native, has won a number of awards from the North Carolina Poetry Society, including its Poet Laureate Award in 1996 and again in 1998. He is the current convenor of The Friday Noon Poets of Chapel Hill, with whom he has read his poetry on Chapel Hill public television. A Pushcart nominee, his poems have appeared in *Asheville Poetry Review, Free Lunch, Southern Poetry Review, The Christian Century, Main Street Rag, Pembroke Magazine, Rattle, New Orleans Review* and other journals. A recent poetry chapbook, *Out After Dark*, was published by Pudding House in 2003.